55 Southwestern States Recipes for Home

By: Kelly Johnson

Table of Contents

Appetizers and Snacks:

- Guacamole with Roasted Corn
- Queso Fundido with Chorizo
- Cilantro Lime Shrimp Skewers
- Salsa Verde Chicken Wings
- Black Bean and Corn Salsa
- Jalapeño Poppers with Cream Cheese and Bacon
- Avocado Hummus

Soups and Stews:

- Chicken Tortilla Soup
- Posole (Hominy and Pork Stew)
- Roasted Tomato and Poblano Soup
- White Bean and Green Chile Chili
- Sopa de Albóndigas (Meatball Soup)

Main Dishes - Meat:

- Carne Asada Tacos
- Green Chile Enchiladas
- Grilled Chipotle Lime Chicken
- CHili Colorado (Red Chili Beef)
- Ancho Chile BBQ Ribs
- Tequila Lime Shrimp Fajitas
- Barbacoa Beef Burritos

Main Dishes - Vegetarian:

- Sweet Potato and Black Bean Enchiladas
- Grilled Portobello Mushroom Tacos
- Spinach and Mushroom Quesadillas
- Southwest Quinoa Salad
- Zucchini and Corn Tamale Pie
- Cactus and Corn Stuffed Peppers

Sides:

- Mexican Street Corn (Elote)
- Cilantro Lime Rice
- Charro Beans
- Roasted Chile Cornbread
- Southwestern Coleslaw
- Chiles Rellenos Casserole

Breakfast and Brunch:

- Huevos Rancheros
- Chorizo and Egg Breakfast Burritos
- Southwest Breakfast Skillet
- Green Chile Cheese Grits
- Breakfast Tostadas
- Sausage and Potato Breakfast Tacos

Dips and Spreads:

- Chipotle Black Bean Dip
- Roasted Red Pepper Hummus
- Hatch Chile Queso
- Spicy Avocado Crema
- Tomatillo Salsa

Salads:

- Grilled Chicken and Avocado Salad
- Nopales (Cactus) Salad
- Black Bean and Corn Salad
- Roasted Poblano Potato Salad
- Jicama and Mango Slaw

Appetizers and Snacks:

- Tres Leches Cake
- Sopapillas with Honey
- Mexican Chocolate Brownies
- Prickly Pear Sorbet
- Churro Ice Cream Sandwiches

- Anise Seed Bizcochitos
- Flan with Caramel Sauce

Appetizers and Snacks:

Guacamole with Roasted Corn

Ingredients:

- 4 ripe avocados, peeled, pitted, and mashed
- 1 cup roasted corn kernels (fresh or frozen)
- 1/2 cup red onion, finely diced
- 1/4 cup fresh cilantro, chopped
- 2 cloves garlic, minced
- 1-2 jalapeños, finely minced (adjust to taste)
- Juice of 2 limes
- Salt and pepper to taste

Instructions:

Roast the Corn:
- If using fresh corn, grill or roast the corn on a stovetop or in the oven until it develops a slight char. If using frozen corn, you can sauté it in a pan until it's lightly browned. Set aside to cool.

Prepare the Avocados:
- Cut the avocados in half, remove the pits, and scoop the flesh into a mixing bowl.

Mash the Avocados:
- Using a fork or potato masher, mash the avocados to your desired consistency. Some prefer a chunky guacamole, while others like it smoother.

Add Lime Juice:
- Squeeze the juice of two limes over the mashed avocados to prevent browning and add a citrusy kick.

Incorporate Roasted Corn:
- Gently fold in the roasted corn kernels into the mashed avocados.

Add Vegetables and Herbs:
- Add the finely diced red onion, minced garlic, chopped cilantro, and finely minced jalapeños to the mixture.

Season to Taste:

- Season the guacamole with salt and pepper. Remember to start with a little and adjust according to your taste preference.

Mix Well:
- Carefully mix all the ingredients together until well combined. Be gentle to avoid mashing the avocados too much.

Chill (Optional):
- For enhanced flavors, refrigerate the guacamole for at least 30 minutes before serving. This also allows the ingredients to meld.

Serve:
- Serve the guacamole with tortilla chips, as a topping for tacos, or alongside your favorite Southwestern dishes.

This Guacamole with Roasted Corn is a delightful twist on the classic guacamole, offering a sweet and smoky flavor from the roasted corn that complements the creamy avocados. Enjoy this versatile dip at parties, gatherings, or as a tasty snack.

Queso Fundido with Chorizo

Ingredients:

- 1 pound (about 450g) Mexican chorizo, casings removed
- 1 tablespoon oil (if needed for cooking chorizo)
- 1 small onion, finely chopped
- 2 cloves garlic, minced
- 2 cups (about 200g) shredded melting cheese, such as Oaxaca, Chihuahua, or Monterey Jack
- 1 cup (about 100g) crumbled queso fresco or feta cheese
- 1-2 jalapeños, finely chopped (optional for heat)
- 1/2 cup chopped fresh cilantro (optional, for garnish)
- Tortilla chips or warm tortillas, for serving

Instructions:

In a skillet over medium heat, cook the chorizo until browned and cooked through. Break it apart with a spoon as it cooks. If the chorizo releases a lot of fat, you can drain excess grease.

Add chopped onions and minced garlic to the chorizo, sautéing until the onions are softened and translucent.

Preheat your oven's broiler.

In a heatproof skillet or oven-safe dish, combine the cooked chorizo mixture, shredded melting cheese, crumbled queso fresco or feta, and chopped jalapeños if using.

Place the skillet or dish under the broiler for 3-5 minutes or until the cheese is melted, bubbly, and slightly browned on top. Keep a close eye on it to prevent burning.

Remove from the oven and garnish with chopped cilantro, if desired.

Serve the Queso Fundido immediately with tortilla chips or warm tortillas for dipping.

Enjoy your Queso Fundido with Chorizo as a flavorful and comforting appetizer for gatherings or a tasty snack!

Queso Fundido with Chorizo

Ingredients:

- 1 pound (about 450g) Mexican chorizo, casing removed
- 1 tablespoon vegetable oil (if needed)
- 1 small onion, finely chopped
- 2 cloves garlic, minced
- 2 cups (about 200g) shredded melting cheese, such as Oaxaca, Chihuahua, or Monterey Jack
- 1 cup (about 100g) crumbled queso fresco or feta cheese
- 1-2 jalapeños, finely chopped (optional, for heat)
- 1/2 cup chopped fresh cilantro (optional, for garnish)
- Tortilla chips or warm tortillas, for serving

Instructions:

In a skillet over medium heat, cook the chorizo until it's browned and cooked through. Break it apart with a spoon as it cooks. If the chorizo releases a lot of fat, you can drain excess grease.

Add chopped onions and minced garlic to the chorizo, sautéing until the onions are softened and translucent.

Preheat your oven's broiler.

In a heatproof skillet or an oven-safe dish, combine the cooked chorizo mixture, shredded melting cheese, crumbled queso fresco or feta, and chopped jalapeños if you want some heat.

Place the skillet or dish under the broiler for 3-5 minutes or until the cheese is melted, bubbly, and slightly browned on top. Keep an eye on it to prevent burning.

Remove from the oven and garnish with chopped cilantro, if desired.

Serve the Queso Fundido with Chorizo immediately with tortilla chips or warm tortillas for dipping.

Enjoy this flavorful and cheesy dish as a fantastic appetizer for parties or a satisfying snack!

Cilantro Lime Shrimp Skewers

Ingredients:

- 1 pound (about 450g) large shrimp, peeled and deveined
- 3 tablespoons olive oil
- 3 tablespoons fresh cilantro, chopped
- 3 cloves garlic, minced
- Zest of 1 lime
- Juice of 2 limes
- 1 teaspoon ground cumin
- 1 teaspoon chili powder (adjust according to your spice preference)
- Salt and black pepper to taste
- Wooden or metal skewers (if using wooden skewers, soak them in water for 30 minutes before using)

Instructions:

In a bowl, whisk together the olive oil, chopped cilantro, minced garlic, lime zest, lime juice, cumin, chili powder, salt, and black pepper.
Add the peeled and deveined shrimp to the marinade. Toss to coat the shrimp evenly. Cover the bowl and let it marinate in the refrigerator for at least 30 minutes, allowing the flavors to meld.
Preheat your grill or grill pan over medium-high heat.
Thread the marinated shrimp onto skewers, making sure to leave space between each shrimp.
Grill the shrimp skewers for 2-3 minutes per side or until they turn pink and opaque. Be careful not to overcook to keep the shrimp tender.
Optional: Brush additional marinade over the shrimp while grilling for extra flavor.
Remove the skewers from the grill and garnish with additional chopped cilantro and lime wedges.
Serve the Cilantro Lime Shrimp Skewers with your favorite side dishes, such as rice, quinoa, or a fresh salad.

Enjoy these flavorful and zesty shrimp skewers as a delightful appetizer or main course!

Salsa Verde Chicken Wings

Ingredients:

For the Chicken Wings:

- 2 pounds (about 900g) chicken wings, split at joints, tips discarded
- Salt and black pepper, to taste
- 1 teaspoon garlic powder
- 1 teaspoon onion powder
- 1 teaspoon smoked paprika
- 1 tablespoon olive oil

For the Salsa Verde Sauce:

- 1 cup salsa verde (store-bought or homemade)
- 2 tablespoons fresh cilantro, chopped
- 2 tablespoons lime juice
- 1 tablespoon honey or agave syrup
- 1 teaspoon ground cumin
- Salt and black pepper, to taste

Instructions:

Preheat your oven to 400°F (200°C).

In a large bowl, toss the chicken wings with salt, black pepper, garlic powder, onion powder, smoked paprika, and olive oil until evenly coated.

Place a wire rack on a baking sheet lined with parchment paper. Arrange the seasoned chicken wings on the rack.

Bake the chicken wings in the preheated oven for about 40-45 minutes or until they are golden brown and crispy, turning them halfway through the cooking time.

While the chicken wings are baking, prepare the Salsa Verde Sauce. In a bowl, mix together salsa verde, chopped cilantro, lime juice, honey or agave syrup, ground cumin, salt, and black pepper.

Once the chicken wings are cooked, transfer them to a large bowl. Pour the Salsa Verde Sauce over the wings and toss until the wings are thoroughly coated in the sauce.

Optionally, you can return the sauced wings to the oven for an additional 5-7 minutes to let the sauce caramelize slightly.
Garnish the wings with additional chopped cilantro and serve them hot with your favorite dipping sauce or alongside celery sticks and ranch dressing.

These Salsa Verde Chicken Wings make a flavorful and zesty appetizer or party dish.

Enjoy!

Black Bean and Corn Salsa

Ingredients:

- 1 can (15 ounces) black beans, drained and rinsed
- 1 cup frozen corn kernels, thawed (you can also use canned or fresh corn)
- 1 cup cherry tomatoes, diced
- 1/2 red onion, finely chopped
- 1/4 cup fresh cilantro, chopped
- 1 jalapeño, seeds removed and finely chopped (adjust to your spice preference)
- Juice of 2 limes
- 2 tablespoons olive oil
- 1 teaspoon ground cumin
- Salt and black pepper, to taste
- Optional: Avocado, diced, for added creaminess

Instructions:

In a large bowl, combine the black beans, corn, cherry tomatoes, red onion, cilantro, and jalapeño.
In a small bowl, whisk together the lime juice, olive oil, ground cumin, salt, and black pepper.
Pour the dressing over the black bean and corn mixture and toss everything together until well combined.
If using diced avocado, gently fold it into the salsa.
Refrigerate the salsa for at least 30 minutes to allow the flavors to meld.
Before serving, give the salsa a quick stir and adjust the seasoning if necessary.
Serve the Black Bean and Corn Salsa as a side dish, dip with tortilla chips, or as a topping for grilled chicken, fish, tacos, or salads.

This Black Bean and Corn Salsa is versatile, colorful, and bursting with flavors. It's perfect for picnics, parties, or as a light and healthy snack. Enjoy!

Jalapeño Poppers with Cream Cheese and Bacon

Ingredients:

- 12 fresh jalapeños
- 8 ounces (about 225g) cream cheese, softened
- 1 cup shredded cheddar or Monterey Jack cheese
- 12 slices of bacon, cut in half
- Toothpicks, for securing the bacon
- Optional: 1 teaspoon garlic powder, onion powder, or other seasonings of your choice

Instructions:

Preheat your oven to 400°F (200°C).
Cut the jalapeños in half lengthwise and remove the seeds and membranes. Use a small spoon or knife to scrape out the seeds and white membranes.
In a bowl, mix together the softened cream cheese, shredded cheddar or Monterey Jack cheese, and any optional seasonings.
Fill each jalapeño half with the cream cheese mixture, ensuring they are well-stuffed.
Wrap each cream cheese-filled jalapeño half with a half-slice of bacon. Secure the bacon with toothpicks if necessary.
Place the bacon-wrapped jalapeños on a baking sheet lined with parchment paper.
Bake in the preheated oven for 20-25 minutes or until the bacon is crispy and the jalapeños are tender.
If you prefer extra crispiness, you can broil the poppers for an additional 1-2 minutes, watching carefully to prevent burning.
Remove from the oven and let them cool slightly before serving.
Optional: Serve with ranch dressing, salsa, or your favorite dipping sauce.

These Jalapeño Poppers with Cream Cheese and Bacon make a delicious and crowd-pleasing appetizer for parties, game days, or any occasion. Enjoy the perfect balance of heat, creaminess, and smoky bacon flavor!

Avocado Hummus

Ingredients:

- 1 can (15 ounces) chickpeas, drained and rinsed
- 2 ripe avocados, peeled and pitted
- 1/4 cup tahini
- 2 cloves garlic, minced
- Juice of 1 lemon
- 3 tablespoons olive oil
- 1/2 teaspoon ground cumin
- Salt and black pepper, to taste
- Optional toppings: chopped cilantro, red pepper flakes, or a drizzle of olive oil

Instructions:

In a food processor, combine the chickpeas, avocados, tahini, minced garlic, lemon juice, olive oil, ground cumin, salt, and black pepper.
Process the mixture until smooth and creamy. If the hummus is too thick, you can add a bit more olive oil or a splash of water to reach your desired consistency.
Taste the hummus and adjust the seasoning, adding more salt, pepper, or lemon juice if needed.
Once the Avocado Hummus is smooth and well-seasoned, transfer it to a serving bowl.
Optional: Garnish the hummus with chopped cilantro, red pepper flakes, or a drizzle of olive oil.
Serve the Avocado Hummus with pita bread, tortilla chips, vegetable sticks, or use it as a spread for sandwiches or wraps.
Store any leftover hummus in an airtight container in the refrigerator. It's best consumed within a few days.

This Avocado Hummus is a delightful twist on the classic hummus, offering a creamy texture and a hint of avocado flavor. Enjoy it as a snack, appetizer, or a tasty addition to your meals!

Soups and Stews:

Chicken Tortilla Soup

Ingredients:

For the Soup:

- 1 tablespoon vegetable oil
- 1 onion, finely chopped
- 2 cloves garlic, minced
- 1 jalapeño, seeds and membranes removed, finely chopped
- 1 teaspoon ground cumin
- 1 teaspoon chili powder
- 1 can (14 ounces) diced tomatoes, undrained
- 4 cups chicken broth
- 1 pound boneless, skinless chicken breasts or thighs, cooked and shredded
- 1 cup corn kernels (fresh, frozen, or canned)
- 1 can (15 ounces) black beans, drained and rinsed
- Salt and black pepper, to taste
- Juice of 1 lime

For Garnish:

- Tortilla strips or tortilla chips
- Shredded cheese (cheddar or Mexican blend)
- Fresh cilantro, chopped
- Avocado, diced
- Lime wedges

Instructions:

In a large pot, heat the vegetable oil over medium heat. Add chopped onions and sauté until softened.
Add minced garlic, chopped jalapeño, ground cumin, and chili powder. Sauté for an additional 1-2 minutes until fragrant.

Pour in the diced tomatoes with their juice and chicken broth. Bring the mixture to a simmer.
Add the shredded chicken, corn, and black beans to the pot. Season with salt and black pepper to taste.
Simmer the soup for about 15-20 minutes to allow the flavors to meld.
Just before serving, add the lime juice and adjust the seasoning if necessary.
Ladle the soup into bowls and garnish with tortilla strips or chips, shredded cheese, chopped cilantro, diced avocado, and lime wedges.
Serve the Chicken Tortilla Soup hot, and enjoy!

Feel free to customize the toppings based on your preferences. This hearty and flavorful

Chicken Tortilla Soup is perfect for a comforting meal, especially on chilly days.

Posole (Hominy and Pork Stew)

Ingredients:

- 2 pounds pork shoulder, cut into chunks
- 1 onion, finely chopped
- 4 cloves garlic, minced
- 2 cans (about 30 ounces each) hominy, drained and rinsed
- 8 cups chicken broth
- 2 dried ancho chilies, stems and seeds removed
- 1 teaspoon dried oregano
- 1 teaspoon ground cumin
- Salt and black pepper, to taste

For Garnish:

- Shredded cabbage
- Radishes, sliced
- Chopped cilantro
- Lime wedges
- Finely chopped onion
- Diced avocado
- Crushed red pepper flakes (optional)

Instructions:

In a large pot, combine pork chunks, chopped onion, minced garlic, chicken broth, ancho chilies, oregano, cumin, salt, and black pepper.
Bring the mixture to a boil and then reduce the heat to simmer. Cover the pot and let it cook for about 1.5 to 2 hours or until the pork is tender and cooked through.
Remove the ancho chilies from the pot, blend them with a little broth until smooth, and return the mixture to the pot. This adds flavor and color to the broth.
Add the hominy to the pot and simmer for an additional 30 minutes.
Adjust the seasoning with more salt and pepper if needed.
Serve the Posole hot in bowls, and let each person customize their bowl with garnishes such as shredded cabbage, sliced radishes, chopped cilantro, lime wedges, chopped onion, diced avocado, and crushed red pepper flakes.

Posole is often enjoyed during festive occasions and celebrations. It's a hearty and satisfying dish with a rich broth and a combination of textures and flavors from the hominy, pork, and various toppings.

Roasted Tomato and Poblano Soup

Ingredients:

- 6 large tomatoes, halved
- 2 poblano peppers, halved and seeds removed
- 1 onion, quartered
- 4 cloves garlic, peeled
- 2 tablespoons olive oil
- Salt and black pepper, to taste
- 4 cups vegetable or chicken broth
- 1 teaspoon ground cumin
- 1 teaspoon dried oregano
- 1/2 teaspoon smoked paprika
- 1/2 cup heavy cream (optional, for added creaminess)
- Fresh cilantro, chopped (for garnish)
- Crumbled queso fresco or shredded cheese (for garnish)
- Tortilla strips or crumbled tortilla chips (for garnish)

Instructions:

Preheat your oven to 400°F (200°C).
Place the halved tomatoes, poblano peppers, quartered onion, and garlic cloves on a baking sheet. Drizzle with olive oil and season with salt and black pepper.
Roast the vegetables in the preheated oven for about 25-30 minutes or until they are softened and slightly charred.
Once roasted, remove the vegetables from the oven and let them cool for a few minutes.
Peel the skin off the poblano peppers if desired, and transfer all the roasted vegetables to a blender or food processor. Blend until smooth.
In a large pot, combine the blended roasted vegetable mixture with vegetable or chicken broth, ground cumin, dried oregano, and smoked paprika. Bring the mixture to a simmer over medium heat.
If using, add the heavy cream to the soup and stir until well combined. Allow the soup to simmer for an additional 10-15 minutes to meld the flavors.
Adjust the seasoning with salt and black pepper to taste.
Ladle the soup into bowls and garnish with chopped cilantro, crumbled queso fresco or shredded cheese, and tortilla strips or crumbled tortilla chips.

Serve the Roasted Tomato and Poblano Soup hot and enjoy!

This soup is a comforting and flavorful option, perfect for cooler days. The roasted vegetables add depth and smokiness to the soup, making it a satisfying and delightful meal.

White Bean and Green Chile Chili

Ingredients:

- 2 tablespoons olive oil
- 1 large onion, diced
- 3 cloves garlic, minced
- 2 cans (15 ounces each) white beans, drained and rinsed (such as cannellini or navy beans)
- 2 cans (4 ounces each) diced green chilies
- 1 teaspoon ground cumin
- 1 teaspoon dried oregano
- 1/2 teaspoon ground coriander
- 1/2 teaspoon smoked paprika
- 4 cups vegetable or chicken broth
- Salt and black pepper, to taste
- 2 cups cooked shredded chicken (optional)
- Fresh cilantro, chopped (for garnish)
- Lime wedges (for serving)
- Shredded cheese, sour cream, or avocado slices (optional, for topping)

Instructions:

In a large pot, heat olive oil over medium heat. Add diced onions and sauté until softened.
Add minced garlic and sauté for an additional 1-2 minutes until fragrant.
Stir in the ground cumin, dried oregano, ground coriander, and smoked paprika. Cook for another 1-2 minutes to toast the spices.
Add the drained white beans, diced green chilies, and shredded chicken (if using) to the pot. Stir to combine.
Pour in the vegetable or chicken broth and bring the mixture to a simmer.
Season the chili with salt and black pepper to taste. Adjust the seasoning as needed.
Allow the chili to simmer for about 20-25 minutes, allowing the flavors to meld.
If you prefer a thicker consistency, you can use a potato masher to partially mash some of the beans.
Serve the White Bean and Green Chile Chili hot, garnished with chopped cilantro and lime wedges.

Optional: Top with shredded cheese, a dollop of sour cream, or slices of avocado for additional flavor.

This chili is versatile and can be customized according to your preferences. It's a comforting and nutritious dish, perfect for chilly days. Enjoy!

Sopa de Albóndigas (Meatball Soup)

Ingredients:

For the Meatballs:

- 1 pound ground beef or a mixture of ground beef and pork
- 1/2 cup white rice, uncooked
- 1/4 cup finely chopped onion
- 2 cloves garlic, minced
- 1/4 cup fresh cilantro, chopped
- 1 egg
- Salt and black pepper, to taste

For the Soup:

- 1 tablespoon vegetable oil
- 1 onion, finely chopped
- 2 carrots, peeled and sliced
- 2 celery stalks, sliced
- 2 cloves garlic, minced
- 1 can (14 ounces) diced tomatoes
- 8 cups beef or chicken broth
- 1 teaspoon dried oregano
- 1 teaspoon ground cumin
- Salt and black pepper, to taste
- 2 medium zucchini, sliced
- 1 cup frozen peas
- Fresh cilantro, chopped (for garnish)
- Lime wedges (for serving)

Instructions:

In a bowl, combine all the meatball ingredients - ground beef, white rice, chopped onion, minced garlic, cilantro, egg, salt, and black pepper. Mix well and form small meatballs, about 1 inch in diameter.

In a large pot, heat vegetable oil over medium heat. Add chopped onions, carrots, celery, and minced garlic. Sauté until the vegetables are softened.

Add diced tomatoes, beef or chicken broth, dried oregano, ground cumin, salt, and black pepper to the pot. Bring the mixture to a simmer.

Gently drop the meatballs into the simmering broth. Allow them to cook for about 10-15 minutes or until cooked through.

Add sliced zucchini and frozen peas to the pot. Simmer for an additional 10 minutes or until the vegetables are tender.

Adjust the seasoning of the soup with salt and pepper if needed.

Serve the Sopa de Albóndigas hot, garnished with fresh cilantro, and with lime wedges on the side for squeezing.

This Meatball Soup is a hearty and satisfying dish, perfect for a comforting meal. Enjoy the combination of flavorful meatballs, vegetables, and aromatic broth in each spoonful!

Main Dishes - Meat:

Carne Asada Tacos

Ingredients:

For the Marinade:

- 1.5 to 2 pounds flank or skirt steak
- 1/4 cup orange juice
- 1/4 cup lime juice
- 3 cloves garlic, minced
- 1/4 cup fresh cilantro, chopped
- 1 teaspoon ground cumin
- 1 teaspoon chili powder
- 1 teaspoon dried oregano
- Salt and black pepper, to taste
- 2 tablespoons vegetable oil

For the Tacos:

- Corn or flour tortillas
- Chopped onions
- Chopped fresh cilantro
- Salsa (your choice of red or green salsa)
- Lime wedges

Instructions:

In a bowl, whisk together orange juice, lime juice, minced garlic, chopped cilantro, ground cumin, chili powder, dried oregano, salt, black pepper, and vegetable oil to make the marinade.

Place the flank or skirt steak in a resealable plastic bag or shallow dish and pour the marinade over the meat. Ensure the steak is well coated. Seal the bag or cover the dish and refrigerate for at least 2 hours, or preferably overnight for more flavor.

Preheat your grill or grill pan to medium-high heat.

Remove the steak from the marinade and let excess marinade drip off. Grill the steak for about 4-6 minutes per side, or until it reaches your desired level of doneness. Flank or skirt steak is best when cooked to medium-rare or medium. Allow the steak to rest for a few minutes before slicing it thinly against the grain.
Warm the tortillas on the grill or in a dry skillet.
Assemble the Carne Asada Tacos by placing slices of the grilled steak on each tortilla.
Top the tacos with chopped onions, chopped fresh cilantro, and your choice of salsa.
Serve the tacos with lime wedges on the side for squeezing.
Enjoy your delicious homemade Carne Asada Tacos!

Feel free to customize your tacos with additional toppings like guacamole, shredded cheese, or sour cream. These tacos are perfect for a casual dinner or a gathering with friends and family.

Green Chile Enchiladas

Ingredients:

For the Filling:

- 2 cups shredded cooked chicken (rotisserie chicken works well)
- 1 cup black beans, drained and rinsed (optional)
- 1 cup corn kernels (fresh, frozen, or canned)
- 1 cup shredded cheese (cheddar, Monterey Jack, or a blend)
- 1/2 cup chopped fresh cilantro
- Salt and black pepper, to taste

For the Green Chile Sauce:

- 2 tablespoons vegetable oil
- 1 onion, finely chopped
- 2 cloves garlic, minced
- 2 cans (4 ounces each) diced green chilies
- 1 teaspoon ground cumin
- 1 teaspoon dried oregano
- 1/2 teaspoon smoked paprika (optional)
- 2 cups chicken or vegetable broth
- Salt and black pepper, to taste

For Assembly:

- 10-12 corn tortillas
- Additional shredded cheese for topping
- Chopped fresh cilantro, for garnish
- Sour cream and sliced green onions (optional, for serving)

Instructions:

Preheat the oven to 375°F (190°C).
In a mixing bowl, combine shredded chicken, black beans, corn, shredded cheese, chopped cilantro, salt, and black pepper. Mix well to create the filling.

In a saucepan, heat vegetable oil over medium heat. Add chopped onions and sauté until softened. Add minced garlic and cook for an additional 1-2 minutes until fragrant.

Stir in diced green chilies, ground cumin, dried oregano, and smoked paprika. Cook for another 1-2 minutes.

Pour in chicken or vegetable broth, and bring the mixture to a simmer. Cook for about 5-7 minutes until the sauce thickens slightly. Season with salt and black pepper to taste.

Assemble the enchiladas by heating the corn tortillas briefly in a dry skillet or microwave to make them pliable.

Spoon a portion of the filling onto each tortilla, roll it up, and place it seam-side down in a baking dish.

Pour the green chile sauce over the rolled tortillas, ensuring they are well coated. Top the enchiladas with additional shredded cheese.

Bake in the preheated oven for about 20-25 minutes or until the cheese is melted and bubbly.

Garnish with chopped fresh cilantro and, if desired, serve with sour cream and sliced green onions.

Serve the Green Chile Enchiladas hot and enjoy!

These enchiladas are a delicious and comforting meal, and you can adjust the filling or toppings according to your preferences. They make for a great family dinner or a dish to share at gatherings.

Grilled Chipotle Lime Chicken

Ingredients:

- 4 boneless, skinless chicken breasts
- 2 tablespoons olive oil
- 2 tablespoons fresh lime juice
- 2 teaspoons chipotle chili powder
- 1 teaspoon ground cumin
- 1 teaspoon garlic powder
- 1 teaspoon onion powder
- 1 teaspoon paprika
- 1 teaspoon dried oregano
- Salt and black pepper, to taste
- Fresh cilantro, chopped (for garnish, optional)
- Lime wedges (for serving)

Instructions:

In a bowl, whisk together olive oil, fresh lime juice, chipotle chili powder, ground cumin, garlic powder, onion powder, paprika, dried oregano, salt, and black pepper to create the marinade.
Place the chicken breasts in a resealable plastic bag or shallow dish. Pour the marinade over the chicken, ensuring that it is well-coated. Seal the bag or cover the dish and refrigerate for at least 30 minutes, or preferably longer for more flavor.
Preheat your grill to medium-high heat.
Remove the chicken from the marinade and let excess marinade drip off.
Grill the chicken breasts for about 6-8 minutes per side or until they reach an internal temperature of 165°F (74°C) and are no longer pink in the center.
Once cooked, remove the chicken from the grill and let it rest for a few minutes.
Optional: Garnish the Grilled Chipotle Lime Chicken with chopped fresh cilantro.
Serve the chicken hot with lime wedges on the side for squeezing.

This Grilled Chipotle Lime Chicken is delicious on its own or can be used in tacos, salads, or wraps. The combination of smoky chipotle and tangy lime creates a flavorful and versatile dish. Enjoy!

Chili Colorado (Red Chili Beef)

Ingredients:

For the Red Chili Sauce:

- 6-8 dried guajillo chilies, stems and seeds removed
- 2 dried ancho chilies, stems and seeds removed
- 2 cloves garlic, minced
- 1 teaspoon ground cumin
- 1 teaspoon dried oregano
- 1/2 teaspoon ground coriander
- 4 cups beef or vegetable broth
- Salt and black pepper, to taste
- 2 tablespoons vegetable oil

For the Beef:

- 2 pounds beef stew meat, cut into bite-sized cubes
- Salt and black pepper, to taste
- 2 tablespoons vegetable oil

Instructions:

In a dry skillet over medium heat, toast the dried guajillo and ancho chilies for a few minutes until they become fragrant. Be careful not to burn them.
Place the toasted chilies in a bowl and cover them with hot water. Let them soak for about 15-20 minutes until they become soft.
Once softened, transfer the chilies to a blender or food processor. Add minced garlic, ground cumin, dried oregano, ground coriander, and a cup of broth. Blend until smooth, adding more broth if needed.
Strain the chili mixture through a fine mesh sieve to remove any pulp and seeds, resulting in a smooth red chili sauce.
In a large pot, heat 2 tablespoons of vegetable oil over medium-high heat. Add the beef cubes, season with salt and black pepper, and brown them on all sides.
Once the beef is browned, pour in the red chili sauce and the remaining broth.
Bring the mixture to a simmer, then reduce the heat to low, cover the pot, and let it simmer for about 2-3 hours or until the beef is tender.
Adjust the seasoning with salt and pepper to taste.

Serve the Chili Colorado over rice or with warm tortillas. Optional toppings include chopped cilantro, diced onions, and lime wedges.

Chile Colorado is a flavorful and comforting dish, perfect for a hearty meal. Enjoy the rich and spicy taste of this classic Mexican recipe!

Ancho Chile BBQ Ribs

Ingredients:

For the Ribs:

- 2 racks of baby back ribs (about 4-5 pounds total)
- Salt and black pepper, to taste
- 2 tablespoons olive oil

For the Ancho Chile BBQ Sauce:

- 2 dried ancho chilies, stems and seeds removed
- 1 cup hot water
- 1 cup ketchup
- 1/2 cup apple cider vinegar
- 1/4 cup brown sugar
- 2 tablespoons molasses
- 2 tablespoons Dijon mustard
- 2 cloves garlic, minced
- 1 teaspoon ground cumin
- 1 teaspoon smoked paprika
- Salt and black pepper, to taste

Instructions:

Preheat your oven to 300°F (150°C).
Season the racks of ribs with salt and black pepper. Drizzle olive oil over the ribs and rub it in to coat them evenly.
Wrap each rack of ribs individually in aluminum foil, creating a sealed packet. Place the foil-wrapped ribs on a baking sheet and bake in the preheated oven for 2.5 to 3 hours, or until the meat is tender and easily pulls away from the bones.
While the ribs are baking, prepare the Ancho Chile BBQ Sauce. In a bowl, soak the dried ancho chilies in hot water for about 15-20 minutes until they are soft.
In a blender or food processor, combine the soaked ancho chilies, ketchup, apple cider vinegar, brown sugar, molasses, Dijon mustard, minced garlic, ground cumin, smoked paprika, salt, and black pepper. Blend until smooth.

Transfer the blended mixture to a saucepan and bring it to a simmer over medium heat. Reduce the heat to low and let it simmer for about 15-20 minutes, stirring occasionally, until the sauce thickens.

Once the ribs are tender, remove them from the foil packets and place them on a preheated grill.

Brush the Ancho Chile BBQ Sauce generously over the ribs, turning and basting as needed to achieve a caramelized and flavorful coating.

Grill the ribs for an additional 15-20 minutes, or until they have a nice char and the sauce is set.

Remove the ribs from the grill, let them rest for a few minutes, then slice and serve.

Enjoy these Ancho Chile BBQ Ribs with your favorite sides for a flavorful and satisfying meal!

Tequila Lime Shrimp Fajitas

Ingredients:

For the Tequila Lime Marinade:

- 1 pound large shrimp, peeled and deveined
- 1/4 cup tequila
- 1/4 cup fresh lime juice
- 2 tablespoons olive oil
- 2 cloves garlic, minced
- 1 teaspoon ground cumin
- 1 teaspoon chili powder
- Salt and black pepper, to taste

For the Fajitas:

- 1 tablespoon vegetable oil
- 1 large onion, thinly sliced
- 1 bell pepper, thinly sliced (use a variety of colors for visual appeal)
- Flour or corn tortillas
- Optional toppings: Salsa, guacamole, sour cream, chopped cilantro, shredded cheese

Instructions:

In a bowl, whisk together tequila, fresh lime juice, olive oil, minced garlic, ground cumin, chili powder, salt, and black pepper to create the marinade.

Add the peeled and deveined shrimp to the marinade, ensuring they are well coated. Cover the bowl and let it marinate in the refrigerator for at least 30 minutes.

Heat vegetable oil in a large skillet over medium-high heat.

Add the sliced onion and bell pepper to the skillet. Sauté for about 5-7 minutes or until the vegetables are softened and slightly caramelized.

Push the vegetables to one side of the skillet and add the marinated shrimp, including the marinade, to the other side. Cook the shrimp for 2-3 minutes per side or until they turn pink and opaque.

Once the shrimp are cooked, combine them with the sautéed vegetables and toss everything together to mix well.
Warm the tortillas in a dry skillet or microwave.
Serve the Tequila Lime Shrimp and sautéed vegetables in warm tortillas.
Optional: Top the fajitas with salsa, guacamole, sour cream, chopped cilantro, or shredded cheese.

Enjoy these Tequila Lime Shrimp Fajitas as a delicious and vibrant meal!

Barbacoa Beef Burritos

Ingredients:

For the Barbacoa Beef:

- 2 pounds beef chuck roast, cut into chunks
- 1 medium onion, finely chopped
- 4 cloves garlic, minced
- 2-3 chipotle peppers in adobo sauce, chopped
- 1 tablespoon ground cumin
- 1 tablespoon dried oregano
- 1 teaspoon ground coriander
- 1 teaspoon smoked paprika
- 1/2 cup beef broth
- Juice of 2 limes
- Salt and black pepper, to taste

For the Burritos:

- Large flour tortillas
- Cooked white or brown rice
- Black beans, drained and rinsed
- Shredded lettuce
- Diced tomatoes
- Shredded cheese (cheddar or Mexican blend)
- Sour cream
- Salsa or pico de gallo
- Fresh cilantro, chopped (for garnish)
- Lime wedges (for serving)

Instructions:

In a blender or food processor, combine chopped onion, minced garlic, chipotle peppers, ground cumin, dried oregano, ground coriander, smoked paprika, beef broth, lime juice, salt, and black pepper. Blend until you have a smooth paste. Place the beef chunks in a slow cooker and pour the blended mixture over them. Make sure the beef is well coated with the marinade.

Cook the beef on low heat for 6-8 hours or until it's tender and easily shreds with a fork.

Once the beef is cooked, shred it using two forks and mix it well with the cooking juices.

Assemble your burritos by placing a large flour tortilla on a flat surface.

Add a layer of cooked rice to the center of the tortilla.

Top the rice with a generous portion of the shredded Barbacoa beef.

Add black beans, shredded lettuce, diced tomatoes, shredded cheese, sour cream, and salsa or pico de gallo.

Garnish with chopped fresh cilantro and fold the sides of the tortilla over the filling, rolling it into a burrito.

Serve the Barbacoa Beef Burritos with lime wedges on the side.

Enjoy these flavorful and hearty Barbacoa Beef Burritos as a delicious and satisfying meal!

Main Dishes - Vegetarian:

Sweet Potato and Black Bean Enchiladas

Ingredients:

For the Filling:

- 2 large sweet potatoes, peeled and diced
- 1 can (15 ounces) black beans, drained and rinsed
- 1 cup corn kernels (fresh, frozen, or canned)
- 1 small red onion, finely chopped
- 2 cloves garlic, minced
- 1 teaspoon ground cumin
- 1 teaspoon chili powder
- Salt and black pepper, to taste
- 1 tablespoon olive oil

For the Enchilada Sauce:

- 2 cans (15 ounces each) red enchilada sauce
- 1 teaspoon ground cumin
- 1 teaspoon chili powder
- Salt and black pepper, to taste

For Assembling:

- 8-10 large flour or corn tortillas
- 2 cups shredded cheese (cheddar, Monterey Jack, or a blend)
- Fresh cilantro, chopped (for garnish)
- Avocado slices (for serving, optional)
- Lime wedges (for serving, optional)
- Sour cream (for serving, optional)

Instructions:

Preheat the oven to 375°F (190°C).

In a large skillet, heat olive oil over medium heat. Add chopped red onion and cook until softened.

Add diced sweet potatoes, minced garlic, ground cumin, chili powder, salt, and black pepper to the skillet. Cook until the sweet potatoes are tender, about 10-12 minutes.

Add black beans and corn to the sweet potato mixture. Cook for an additional 3-5 minutes to heat through.

In a separate bowl, mix together the enchilada sauce, ground cumin, chili powder, salt, and black pepper.

Spread a small amount of the enchilada sauce in the bottom of a baking dish.

Assemble the enchiladas by spooning the sweet potato and black bean mixture into each tortilla, rolling them up, and placing them seam side down in the baking dish.

Pour the remaining enchilada sauce over the rolled tortillas, ensuring they are well coated.

Sprinkle shredded cheese over the top.

Bake in the preheated oven for about 20-25 minutes or until the enchiladas are heated through, and the cheese is melted and bubbly.

Garnish with chopped cilantro and serve with avocado slices, lime wedges, and sour cream if desired.

These Sweet Potato and Black Bean Enchiladas are a flavorful and nutritious option for a vegetarian meal. Enjoy the combination of sweet potatoes, black beans, and spices wrapped in a tortilla and baked to perfection!

Grilled Portobello Mushroom Tacos

Ingredients:

For the Grilled Portobello Mushrooms:

- 4 large portobello mushrooms, cleaned and stems removed
- 2 tablespoons olive oil
- 2 tablespoons balsamic vinegar
- 2 cloves garlic, minced
- 1 teaspoon ground cumin
- 1 teaspoon chili powder
- Salt and black pepper, to taste

For the Toppings and Assembly:

- 8 small corn or flour tortillas
- Shredded lettuce or cabbage
- Diced tomatoes
- Sliced red onion
- Fresh cilantro, chopped
- Lime wedges
- Avocado slices
- Sour cream or Greek yogurt (optional)
- Salsa or hot sauce (optional)

Instructions:

In a bowl, whisk together olive oil, balsamic vinegar, minced garlic, ground cumin, chili powder, salt, and black pepper to create the marinade.
Brush the cleaned portobello mushrooms with the marinade, ensuring they are well coated. Let them marinate for at least 15-20 minutes.
Preheat a grill or grill pan over medium-high heat.
Grill the portobello mushrooms for about 4-5 minutes per side, or until they are tender and have nice grill marks.
While the mushrooms are grilling, warm the tortillas on the grill or in a dry skillet.
Remove the portobello mushrooms from the grill and slice them into strips.
Assemble the tacos by placing a generous portion of grilled portobello strips on each tortilla.

Top with shredded lettuce or cabbage, diced tomatoes, sliced red onion, and chopped cilantro.
Serve the Grilled Portobello Mushroom Tacos with lime wedges, avocado slices, and optional toppings like sour cream or Greek yogurt, and salsa or hot sauce. Enjoy these flavorful and satisfying vegetarian tacos!

These Grilled Portobello Mushroom Tacos are not only delicious but also versatile. Feel free to customize them with your favorite toppings and sauces for a tasty and satisfying meatless meal.

Southwest Quinoa Salad

Ingredients:

For the Salad:

- 1 cup quinoa, rinsed and cooked according to package instructions
- 1 can (15 ounces) black beans, drained and rinsed
- 1 cup corn kernels (fresh, frozen, or canned)
- 1 red bell pepper, diced
- 1 orange or yellow bell pepper, diced
- 1 cup cherry tomatoes, halved
- 1/2 red onion, finely chopped
- 1/4 cup fresh cilantro, chopped

For the Dressing:

- 3 tablespoons olive oil
- 2 tablespoons lime juice
- 1 teaspoon ground cumin
- 1 teaspoon chili powder
- 1/2 teaspoon garlic powder
- Salt and black pepper, to taste

Optional Toppings:

- Avocado slices
- Jalapeño slices
- Shredded cheese (cheddar or Mexican blend)
- Sour cream or Greek yogurt

Instructions:

Cook quinoa according to package instructions. Once cooked, allow it to cool to room temperature.
In a large bowl, combine the cooked quinoa, black beans, corn, diced bell peppers, cherry tomatoes, red onion, and chopped cilantro.

In a small bowl, whisk together olive oil, lime juice, ground cumin, chili powder, garlic powder, salt, and black pepper to create the dressing.

Pour the dressing over the quinoa mixture and toss everything until well combined.

Chill the Southwest Quinoa Salad in the refrigerator for at least 30 minutes to allow the flavors to meld.

Just before serving, adjust the seasoning if needed and toss the salad again.

Optional: Top the salad with avocado slices, jalapeño slices, shredded cheese, and a dollop of sour cream or Greek yogurt.

Serve the Southwest Quinoa Salad as a refreshing and nutritious side dish or a light main course.

This Southwest Quinoa Salad is not only delicious but also versatile. Feel free to customize it by adding your favorite ingredients or adjusting the dressing to suit your taste. Enjoy this colorful and healthy salad!

Zucchini and Corn Tamale Pie

Ingredients:

For the Filling:

- 2 tablespoons vegetable oil
- 1 large onion, finely chopped
- 3 cloves garlic, minced
- 2 medium zucchini, diced
- 1 cup corn kernels (fresh, frozen, or canned)
- 1 red bell pepper, diced
- 1 teaspoon ground cumin
- 1 teaspoon chili powder
- Salt and black pepper, to taste
- 1 can (15 ounces) black beans, drained and rinsed
- 1 cup shredded cheese (cheddar or Mexican blend)

For the Cornmeal Crust:

- 1 cup cornmeal
- 1 cup all-purpose flour
- 1 tablespoon baking powder
- 1/2 teaspoon salt
- 1 cup milk
- 1/4 cup vegetable oil
- 2 tablespoons honey or sugar

Instructions:

Preheat the oven to 375°F (190°C).

In a large skillet, heat vegetable oil over medium heat. Add chopped onions and garlic, and sauté until softened.

Add diced zucchini, corn, diced red bell pepper, ground cumin, chili powder, salt, and black pepper to the skillet. Cook for about 5-7 minutes, or until the vegetables are tender.

Stir in the black beans and cook for an additional 2-3 minutes until everything is well combined. Remove from heat.

In a separate bowl, combine cornmeal, all-purpose flour, baking powder, and salt to make the cornmeal crust.

In another bowl, whisk together milk, vegetable oil, and honey (or sugar).

Add the wet ingredients to the dry ingredients and stir until just combined.

Pour half of the cornmeal batter into a greased baking dish, spreading it evenly.

Spoon the zucchini and corn filling over the cornmeal crust.

Sprinkle shredded cheese over the filling.

Pour the remaining cornmeal batter over the filling, spreading it to cover the vegetables.

Bake in the preheated oven for about 25-30 minutes or until the top is golden and a toothpick inserted into the cornmeal crust comes out clean.

Let the Zucchini and Corn Tamale Pie cool for a few minutes before slicing and serving.

This Zucchini and Corn Tamale Pie is a flavorful and satisfying vegetarian dish that's perfect for a cozy dinner. Enjoy the combination of zucchini, corn, and a tasty cornmeal crust!

Cactus and Corn Stuffed Peppers

Ingredients:

- 4 large bell peppers (any color), halved and seeds removed
- 1 tablespoon vegetable oil
- 1 cup diced cactus pads (nopales), cleaned and prepared
- 1 cup corn kernels (fresh, frozen, or canned)
- 1 small onion, finely chopped
- 2 cloves garlic, minced
- 1 teaspoon ground cumin
- 1 teaspoon chili powder
- Salt and black pepper, to taste
- 1 can (15 ounces) black beans, drained and rinsed
- 1 cup cooked rice (white or brown)
- 1 cup shredded cheese (cheddar, Monterey Jack, or Mexican blend)
- Fresh cilantro, chopped (for garnish)
- Lime wedges (for serving)

Instructions:

Preheat the oven to 375°F (190°C).
Place the halved bell peppers in a baking dish.
In a large skillet, heat vegetable oil over medium heat. Add diced cactus pads and cook for about 5-7 minutes, or until they are tender.
Add corn kernels, chopped onion, minced garlic, ground cumin, chili powder, salt, and black pepper to the skillet. Cook for an additional 5 minutes, allowing the flavors to meld.
Stir in black beans and cooked rice. Cook for another 2-3 minutes until everything is well combined.
Spoon the cactus and corn mixture into the halved bell peppers, pressing down gently to pack the filling.
Sprinkle shredded cheese over the top of each stuffed pepper.
Cover the baking dish with aluminum foil and bake in the preheated oven for 25-30 minutes, or until the peppers are tender.
Remove the foil and bake for an additional 5-7 minutes or until the cheese is melted and bubbly.
Garnish the Cactus and Corn Stuffed Peppers with chopped fresh cilantro.

Serve the stuffed peppers hot with lime wedges on the side for squeezing.

This unique and delicious dish is a great way to enjoy the flavors of cactus and corn in a comforting stuffed pepper. Enjoy!

Sides:

Mexican Street Corn (Elote)

Ingredients:

- 4 ears of fresh corn, husked
- 1/4 cup mayonnaise
- 1/4 cup sour cream
- 1/2 cup crumbled cotija cheese (or feta cheese)
- 1 teaspoon chili powder (adjust to taste)
- 1/2 teaspoon smoked paprika
- 1 clove garlic, minced
- Fresh cilantro, chopped (for garnish)
- Lime wedges (for serving)

Instructions:

Preheat a grill or grill pan over medium-high heat.

Grill the corn on all sides until it has nice grill marks and is cooked through, about 10-15 minutes.

In a small bowl, mix together mayonnaise, sour cream, crumbled cotija cheese, chili powder, smoked paprika, and minced garlic.

Once the corn is grilled, brush each ear with the mayonnaise and cheese mixture, making sure to coat each side evenly.

Sprinkle extra crumbled cotija cheese, chili powder, and chopped cilantro over the top of each corn cob.

Serve the Mexican Street Corn hot with lime wedges on the side for squeezing.

Enjoy the rich and flavorful combination of creamy, cheesy, and tangy goodness that makes Mexican Street Corn a beloved street food favorite!

Cilantro Lime Rice

Ingredients:

- 1 cup long-grain white rice
- 2 cups water or vegetable broth
- 1 tablespoon olive oil or butter
- 1 teaspoon salt
- Zest of 1 lime
- 2 tablespoons fresh lime juice
- 1/4 cup fresh cilantro, finely chopped

Instructions:

Rinse the rice under cold water until the water runs clear to remove excess starch.

In a medium saucepan, combine the rinsed rice, water or vegetable broth, olive oil or butter, and salt.

Bring the mixture to a boil over medium-high heat. Once boiling, reduce the heat to low, cover the saucepan with a tight-fitting lid, and simmer for 15-18 minutes or until the rice is cooked and the liquid is absorbed.

While the rice is cooking, zest the lime and chop the fresh cilantro.

Once the rice is cooked, fluff it with a fork.

Add the lime zest, lime juice, and chopped cilantro to the cooked rice. Gently toss the rice to combine.

Taste the rice and adjust the seasoning with additional salt or lime juice if desired.

Cover the saucepan with the lid and let the Cilantro Lime Rice sit for a few minutes to allow the flavors to meld.

Serve the Cilantro Lime Rice as a side dish with your favorite Mexican or Southwestern meals.

This Cilantro Lime Rice is a versatile and tasty accompaniment to dishes like burritos, tacos, fajitas, or grilled chicken. Enjoy the bright and citrusy flavors!

Charro Beans

Ingredients:

- 2 cups dried pinto beans
- 6 cups water (for soaking)
- 1 tablespoon vegetable oil
- 1/2 pound bacon, chopped
- 1/2 pound Mexican chorizo, casing removed
- 1 onion, finely chopped
- 3 cloves garlic, minced
- 2 jalapeño peppers, seeded and finely chopped
- 1 can (14 ounces) diced tomatoes (with juices)
- 1/4 cup fresh cilantro, chopped
- 1 teaspoon ground cumin
- 1 teaspoon chili powder
- Salt and black pepper, to taste
- 4 cups chicken broth

Instructions:

Rinse the dried pinto beans under cold water. Place them in a large bowl and cover with about 6 cups of water. Allow the beans to soak overnight or for at least 6 hours.

After soaking, drain and rinse the beans.

In a large pot, heat the vegetable oil over medium heat. Add the chopped bacon and cook until it starts to brown.

Add the Mexican chorizo to the pot, breaking it up with a spoon and cooking until browned.

Add the chopped onion, minced garlic, and jalapeño peppers to the pot. Sauté until the vegetables are softened.

Stir in the soaked and drained pinto beans, diced tomatoes (with juices), chopped cilantro, ground cumin, chili powder, salt, and black pepper.

Pour in the chicken broth, ensuring that the beans are covered with liquid.

Bring the mixture to a boil, then reduce the heat to low, cover the pot, and simmer for about 1.5 to 2 hours, or until the beans are tender. Stir occasionally and add more broth if needed to maintain the desired consistency.

Taste and adjust the seasoning as needed.

Serve the Charro Beans hot as a side dish to your favorite Mexican meals.

Charro Beans are delicious on their own or as a side dish with rice, tacos, or grilled meats. Enjoy the rich and savory flavors of this classic Mexican dish!

Roasted Chile Cornbread

Ingredients:

- 1 cup cornmeal
- 1 cup all-purpose flour
- 1 tablespoon baking powder
- 1/2 teaspoon baking soda
- 1/2 teaspoon salt
- 1 cup buttermilk
- 2 large eggs
- 1/4 cup unsalted butter, melted
- 1 cup corn kernels (fresh, frozen, or canned)
- 1 cup shredded cheddar cheese
- 1/2 cup roasted and diced green chilies (canned or fresh-roasted)
- 2 tablespoons honey (optional, for sweetness)

Instructions:

Preheat the oven to 375°F (190°C). Grease a baking dish (8 or 9-inch square or round) or cast-iron skillet.

In a large bowl, whisk together cornmeal, all-purpose flour, baking powder, baking soda, and salt.

In a separate bowl, whisk together buttermilk, eggs, and melted butter.

Add the wet ingredients to the dry ingredients, stirring until just combined.

Gently fold in corn kernels, shredded cheddar cheese, diced green chilies, and honey (if using).

Pour the batter into the prepared baking dish or skillet, spreading it evenly.

Bake in the preheated oven for 25-30 minutes, or until the top is golden brown and a toothpick inserted into the center comes out clean.

Allow the Roasted Chile Cornbread to cool for a few minutes before slicing and serving.

This flavorful Roasted Chile Cornbread is perfect for serving alongside soups, stews, chili, or as a side dish to your favorite meals. Enjoy the combination of cornmeal, cheese, and roasted chilies for a delightful twist on classic cornbread!

Southwestern Coleslaw

Ingredients:

For the Coleslaw:

- 1 small head of green cabbage, finely shredded
- 1 large carrot, grated
- 1 red bell pepper, thinly sliced
- 1/2 red onion, thinly sliced
- 1 cup corn kernels (fresh, frozen, or canned)
- 1/4 cup fresh cilantro, chopped

For the Dressing:

- 1/2 cup mayonnaise
- 2 tablespoons sour cream
- 2 tablespoons lime juice
- 1 teaspoon ground cumin
- 1 teaspoon chili powder
- 1/2 teaspoon smoked paprika
- Salt and black pepper, to taste

Instructions:

In a large bowl, combine shredded cabbage, grated carrot, sliced red bell pepper, sliced red onion, corn kernels, and chopped cilantro.
In a separate bowl, whisk together mayonnaise, sour cream, lime juice, ground cumin, chili powder, smoked paprika, salt, and black pepper to create the dressing.
Pour the dressing over the coleslaw ingredients.
Toss everything together until the vegetables are evenly coated with the dressing.
Adjust the seasoning to taste, adding more salt, pepper, or lime juice if needed.
Cover the bowl and refrigerate the Southwestern Coleslaw for at least 30 minutes to allow the flavors to meld.
Just before serving, toss the coleslaw again to ensure an even coating of the dressing.
Serve the Southwestern Coleslaw as a refreshing and flavorful side dish.

This Southwestern Coleslaw is a perfect accompaniment to grilled meats, tacos, sandwiches, or as a side dish for barbecues and picnics. Enjoy the crunchy texture and zesty flavors!

Chiles Rellenos Casserole

Ingredients:

- 4 large poblano peppers
- 1 tablespoon vegetable oil
- 1 onion, finely chopped
- 2 cloves garlic, minced
- 1 pound ground beef or turkey
- 1 teaspoon ground cumin
- 1 teaspoon chili powder
- Salt and black pepper, to taste
- 1 can (14 ounces) diced tomatoes, drained
- 1 cup shredded Monterey Jack or Mexican blend cheese
- 1 cup shredded cheddar cheese
- 4 large eggs
- 1 cup milk
- 1/2 cup all-purpose flour
- 1 teaspoon baking powder

Instructions:

Preheat the oven to 375°F (190°C). Grease a 9x13-inch baking dish.
Roast the poblano peppers by placing them directly over an open flame or under the broiler until the skins blister and char. Allow them to cool, then peel off the skins, remove the seeds, and cut them into strips.
In a large skillet, heat vegetable oil over medium heat. Add chopped onion and minced garlic, cooking until softened.
Add ground beef or turkey to the skillet and cook until browned. Drain excess fat.
Season the meat with ground cumin, chili powder, salt, and black pepper. Stir in the diced tomatoes and cook for an additional 2-3 minutes.
Spread half of the meat mixture into the prepared baking dish.
Layer half of the roasted poblano strips over the meat mixture.
Sprinkle half of the Monterey Jack or Mexican blend cheese and half of the cheddar cheese over the poblano strips.
Repeat the layers with the remaining meat mixture, poblano strips, and cheeses.
In a bowl, whisk together eggs, milk, all-purpose flour, and baking powder until well combined.

Pour the egg mixture over the layers in the baking dish.
Bake in the preheated oven for about 35-40 minutes or until the top is golden brown and the casserole is set.
Allow the Chiles Rellenos Casserole to cool for a few minutes before slicing and serving.

This Chiles Rellenos Casserole captures the essence of the classic dish in an easy and convenient baked form. Enjoy the layers of roasted poblanos, seasoned meat, and cheesy goodness!

Breakfast and Brunch:

Huevos Rancheros

Ingredients:

For the Ranchero Sauce:

- 2 tablespoons vegetable oil
- 1 onion, finely chopped
- 2 cloves garlic, minced
- 1 can (14 ounces) crushed tomatoes
- 1-2 jalapeño peppers, finely chopped (adjust to taste)
- 1 teaspoon ground cumin
- 1 teaspoon chili powder
- Salt and black pepper, to taste

For the Huevos Rancheros:

- 4 large eggs
- 4 corn tortillas
- 1 can (15 ounces) black beans, warmed
- 1 cup shredded cheese (cheddar or Mexican blend)
- Fresh cilantro, chopped (for garnish)
- Avocado slices (optional, for serving)
- Lime wedges (optional, for serving)

Instructions:

In a skillet, heat vegetable oil over medium heat. Add chopped onion and sauté until softened.
Add minced garlic and jalapeño peppers to the skillet, cooking for an additional minute.
Stir in crushed tomatoes, ground cumin, chili powder, salt, and black pepper.
Simmer the sauce for about 10-15 minutes, allowing the flavors to meld and the sauce to thicken.
While the sauce is simmering, warm the tortillas in a dry skillet or microwave.
In another skillet, fry the eggs to your desired doneness.

To assemble, place a warmed tortilla on a plate. Spread a spoonful of warmed black beans over the tortilla.
Carefully place a fried egg on top of the beans.
Spoon the Ranchero sauce over the egg, covering it generously.
Sprinkle shredded cheese over the sauce.
Garnish with chopped cilantro and add avocado slices if desired.
Serve the Huevos Rancheros hot, with lime wedges on the side.

Enjoy this classic Mexican breakfast dish, Huevos Rancheros, with its delicious combination of flavors and textures!

Chorizo and Egg Breakfast Burritos

Ingredients:

- 1/2 pound chorizo sausage, casing removed
- 4 large eggs, beaten
- Salt and black pepper, to taste
- 4 large flour tortillas
- 1 cup shredded cheese (cheddar, Monterey Jack, or Mexican blend)
- 1 cup diced tomatoes
- 1/2 cup diced onions
- 1/4 cup chopped fresh cilantro
- Salsa, for serving
- Avocado slices, for serving (optional)
- Lime wedges, for serving (optional)

Instructions:

In a skillet over medium heat, cook the chorizo sausage, breaking it into crumbles with a spoon as it cooks. Cook until browned and cooked through.
Push the cooked chorizo to one side of the skillet and add beaten eggs to the other side. Season the eggs with salt and black pepper.
Scramble the eggs and cook until they are just set.
Mix the cooked chorizo with the scrambled eggs in the skillet. Remove from heat.
Warm the flour tortillas in a dry skillet or microwave.
Spoon the chorizo and egg mixture onto the center of each tortilla.
Sprinkle shredded cheese over the top of the chorizo and eggs.
Add diced tomatoes, diced onions, and chopped cilantro on top of the cheese.
Fold the sides of the tortillas over the filling and roll them up to form burritos.
Serve the Chorizo and Egg Breakfast Burritos with salsa on the side.
Optional: Garnish with avocado slices and serve with lime wedges.

Enjoy these flavorful Chorizo and Egg Breakfast Burritos for a satisfying and delicious breakfast or brunch!

Southwest Breakfast Skillet

Ingredients:

- 1 tablespoon vegetable oil
- 1 small onion, diced
- 1 bell pepper, diced (any color)
- 1 jalapeño, seeded and finely chopped
- 1 cup diced tomatoes (fresh or canned)
- 1 cup black beans, drained and rinsed
- 1 teaspoon ground cumin
- 1 teaspoon chili powder
- Salt and black pepper, to taste
- 4 large eggs
- 1 cup shredded cheese (cheddar, Monterey Jack, or Mexican blend)
- Fresh cilantro, chopped (for garnish)
- Avocado slices (optional, for serving)
- Lime wedges (optional, for serving)

Instructions:

Heat vegetable oil in a large skillet over medium heat.
Add diced onion, bell pepper, and jalapeño to the skillet. Sauté until the vegetables are softened.
Stir in diced tomatoes, black beans, ground cumin, chili powder, salt, and black pepper. Cook for an additional 3-5 minutes until the flavors meld.
Make four wells in the vegetable mixture and crack an egg into each well.
Sprinkle shredded cheese over the top of the skillet.
Cover the skillet and cook until the eggs are cooked to your liking and the cheese is melted, about 5-7 minutes.
Remove the skillet from heat and garnish with chopped fresh cilantro.
Optional: Serve the Southwest Breakfast Skillet with avocado slices and lime wedges on the side.
Spoon the mixture onto plates, ensuring each serving includes a portion of eggs, vegetables, and cheese.

This Southwest Breakfast Skillet is a delicious and filling breakfast that can be served with warm tortillas or crusty bread. Enjoy the bold flavors of the Southwest in this easy and satisfying one-pan dish!

Green Chile Cheese Grits

Ingredients:

- 1 cup stone-ground grits
- 4 cups water
- 1 teaspoon salt
- 1/2 cup unsalted butter
- 1 cup shredded sharp cheddar cheese
- 1 can (4 ounces) diced green chiles, drained
- 1/4 cup chopped fresh cilantro (optional, for garnish)
- Lime wedges (optional, for serving)

Instructions:

In a medium-sized saucepan, bring 4 cups of water to a boil.
Slowly whisk in the grits, stirring constantly to prevent lumps.
Reduce the heat to low, cover the saucepan, and simmer the grits for about 20-25 minutes, stirring occasionally, until they are thick and creamy.
Stir in the salt, unsalted butter, shredded cheddar cheese, and diced green chiles. Continue to stir until the cheese and butter are melted, and the green chiles are well distributed.
Optional: Add chopped fresh cilantro and stir to incorporate.
Adjust the seasoning if needed, adding more salt or pepper to taste.
Serve the Green Chile Cheese Grits hot, garnished with additional cheese, cilantro, and lime wedges if desired.

Enjoy these Green Chile Cheese Grits as a delicious and comforting side dish for breakfast, brunch, or any meal. The combination of creamy grits, sharp cheddar, and the mild heat of green chiles creates a flavorful and satisfying dish!

Breakfast Tostadas

Ingredients:

- 4 corn or flour tortillas
- 1 tablespoon vegetable oil
- 4 large eggs
- Salt and black pepper, to taste
- 1 cup black beans, warmed
- 1 cup diced tomatoes
- 1 avocado, sliced
- 1/2 cup shredded cheese (cheddar, Monterey Jack, or Mexican blend)
- Fresh cilantro, chopped (for garnish)
- Salsa or hot sauce (optional, for serving)

Instructions:

Preheat the oven to 375°F (190°C).
Brush both sides of the tortillas with vegetable oil. Place them on a baking sheet and bake in the preheated oven for about 10 minutes or until they are crispy and lightly browned.
While the tortillas are baking, heat a skillet over medium heat. Crack the eggs into the skillet and cook to your desired doneness. Season with salt and black pepper.
Once the tortillas are ready, assemble the tostadas. Spread a layer of warmed black beans on each tortilla.
Place a cooked egg on top of the beans on each tostada.
Add diced tomatoes, sliced avocado, and shredded cheese over the eggs.
Optional: Drizzle salsa or hot sauce over the tostadas for an extra kick.
Garnish with chopped fresh cilantro.
Serve the Breakfast Tostadas immediately while the tortillas are still crispy.

Enjoy these flavorful Breakfast Tostadas as a satisfying and customizable morning meal. The combination of crispy tortillas, creamy black beans, eggs, and fresh toppings creates a delicious breakfast experience!

Sausage and Potato Breakfast Tacos

Ingredients:

- 1 pound breakfast sausage
- 2 cups diced potatoes (russet or Yukon gold)
- 1/2 cup diced onion
- 1/2 cup diced bell pepper (any color)
- 1 teaspoon vegetable oil
- Salt and black pepper, to taste
- 8 small flour or corn tortillas
- 8 large eggs
- 1 cup shredded cheese (cheddar, Monterey Jack, or Mexican blend)
- Fresh cilantro, chopped (for garnish)
- Salsa or hot sauce (optional, for serving)

Instructions:

In a large skillet, cook the breakfast sausage over medium heat, breaking it up with a spoon as it cooks. Cook until browned and cooked through. Remove excess fat if needed.
In the same skillet, add vegetable oil and sauté diced potatoes, diced onion, and diced bell pepper. Season with salt and black pepper. Cook until the potatoes are tender and golden brown.
Push the potato mixture to one side of the skillet and crack the eggs into the other side. Scramble the eggs until they are just set.
Mix the scrambled eggs with the potato mixture and cooked sausage in the skillet. Ensure everything is well combined.
Warm the tortillas in a dry skillet or microwave.
Spoon the sausage and potato mixture onto each tortilla.
Sprinkle shredded cheese over the top of each taco.
Optional: Garnish with chopped fresh cilantro and drizzle with salsa or hot sauce for extra flavor.
Serve the Sausage and Potato Breakfast Tacos hot.

Enjoy these hearty and flavorful breakfast tacos, perfect for a satisfying and filling morning meal!

Dips and Spreads:

Chipotle Black Bean Dip

Ingredients:

- 2 cans (15 ounces each) black beans, drained and rinsed
- 2 chipotle peppers in adobo sauce, plus 1 tablespoon adobo sauce
- 2 cloves garlic, minced
- 1/4 cup fresh cilantro, chopped
- 1 teaspoon ground cumin
- 1 teaspoon chili powder
- 1/2 teaspoon onion powder
- Juice of 1 lime
- Salt and black pepper, to taste
- 1/4 cup olive oil
- 1 cup shredded cheese (cheddar, Monterey Jack, or Mexican blend)
- Additional cilantro, chopped (for garnish)
- Tortilla chips or vegetable sticks (for serving)

Instructions:

In a food processor, combine black beans, chipotle peppers, adobo sauce, minced garlic, chopped cilantro, ground cumin, chili powder, onion powder, lime juice, salt, and black pepper.
Pulse the ingredients until the mixture is smooth, scraping down the sides of the processor bowl as needed.
With the food processor running, gradually add the olive oil until the dip reaches your desired consistency.
Taste the dip and adjust the seasoning if needed.
Stir in the shredded cheese until well combined.
Transfer the Chipotle Black Bean Dip to a serving bowl.
Garnish with additional chopped cilantro.
Serve the dip with tortilla chips or vegetable sticks.

This Chipotle Black Bean Dip is perfect for parties, game day, or anytime you crave a flavorful and spicy dip. Enjoy the bold and smoky flavors of chipotle paired with the creaminess of black beans!

Roasted Red Pepper Hummus

Ingredients:

- 1 can (15 ounces) chickpeas (garbanzo beans), drained and rinsed
- 1/3 cup tahini (sesame paste)
- 1/4 cup extra-virgin olive oil, plus extra for drizzling
- 1/4 cup fresh lemon juice (about 1 large lemon)
- 2 cloves garlic, minced
- 1/2 cup roasted red peppers, drained (store-bought or homemade)
- 1 teaspoon ground cumin
- 1/2 teaspoon smoked paprika
- Salt, to taste
- Water, as needed for texture
- Optional toppings: chopped fresh parsley, additional roasted red peppers, or a sprinkle of paprika

Instructions:

In a food processor, combine chickpeas, tahini, olive oil, lemon juice, minced garlic, roasted red peppers, ground cumin, smoked paprika, and a pinch of salt. Process the ingredients until smooth, scraping down the sides of the food processor as needed.
If the hummus is too thick, add water, one tablespoon at a time, until you reach your desired consistency.
Taste the hummus and adjust the seasoning, adding more salt or lemon juice if needed.
Transfer the Roasted Red Pepper Hummus to a serving bowl.
Drizzle with extra-virgin olive oil and garnish with optional toppings like chopped fresh parsley, additional roasted red peppers, or a sprinkle of paprika.
Serve the hummus with pita bread, crackers, vegetable sticks, or as a spread for sandwiches.

Enjoy this Roasted Red Pepper Hummus as a delicious and colorful appetizer or snack!

Hatch Chile Queso

Ingredients:

- 1 tablespoon olive oil
- 1/2 cup finely chopped onion
- 2 cloves garlic, minced
- 2 tablespoons all-purpose flour
- 1 cup milk
- 8 ounces cream cheese, softened
- 2 cups shredded Monterey Jack cheese
- 1 cup shredded sharp cheddar cheese
- 1 cup diced Hatch chiles (fresh or roasted, peeled, and seeded)
- Salt and black pepper, to taste
- 1/4 cup chopped fresh cilantro (optional, for garnish)
- Tortilla chips or bread slices (for serving)

Instructions:

In a medium saucepan, heat olive oil over medium heat. Add chopped onion and cook until softened.
Add minced garlic to the saucepan and cook for an additional minute.
Sprinkle flour over the onion and garlic, stirring constantly to create a roux. Cook for 1-2 minutes to remove the raw flour taste.
Gradually whisk in milk, making sure there are no lumps. Continue to cook and whisk until the mixture thickens.
Reduce heat to low and add cream cheese, Monterey Jack, and cheddar cheese to the saucepan. Stir until the cheeses are melted and the mixture is smooth.
Fold in diced Hatch chiles, and season with salt and black pepper to taste. Cook for an additional 2-3 minutes, allowing the flavors to meld.
Optional: Stir in chopped fresh cilantro for added freshness.
Transfer the Hatch Chile Queso to a serving bowl.
Serve the queso warm with tortilla chips or slices of bread for dipping.

Enjoy the creamy and spicy goodness of Hatch Chile Queso as a party appetizer or snack. It's perfect for gatherings and pairs well with a variety of dippables!

Spicy Avocado Crema

Ingredients:

- 2 ripe avocados, peeled and pitted
- 1/2 cup sour cream
- 1-2 tablespoons fresh lime juice
- 1 clove garlic, minced
- 1-2 teaspoons hot sauce (adjust to taste)
- 1/4 cup fresh cilantro, chopped
- Salt and black pepper, to taste

Instructions:

In a blender or food processor, combine the ripe avocados, sour cream, fresh lime juice, minced garlic, hot sauce, and chopped cilantro.
Blend the ingredients until smooth and creamy. If the crema is too thick, you can add a bit of water or additional lime juice to achieve your desired consistency.
Season the Spicy Avocado Crema with salt and black pepper to taste. Adjust the level of spiciness by adding more hot sauce if desired.
Transfer the crema to a serving bowl.
Refrigerate for at least 30 minutes before serving to allow the flavors to meld.
Serve the Spicy Avocado Crema as a dip for tortilla chips, a topping for tacos, or a spread for sandwiches and wraps.

Enjoy the creamy and spicy goodness of this Spicy Avocado Crema, adding a burst of flavor to your favorite dishes!

Tomatillo Salsa

Ingredients:

- 1 pound fresh tomatillos, husked and washed
- 1-2 jalapeño peppers (adjust to taste)
- 1/2 cup chopped onion
- 2 cloves garlic, minced
- 1/2 cup fresh cilantro, chopped
- Juice of 1 lime
- Salt, to taste

Instructions:

Preheat the broiler in your oven.
Place the tomatillos and jalapeño peppers on a baking sheet. Broil for 5-7 minutes, turning them occasionally until the skins are blistered and slightly charred.
Allow the tomatillos and peppers to cool slightly.
Remove the stems from the jalapeños and cut the tomatillos in half.
In a blender or food processor, combine the roasted tomatillos, jalapeños, chopped onion, minced garlic, cilantro, lime juice, and a pinch of salt.
Blend until the mixture reaches your desired consistency. If you prefer a chunkier salsa, pulse the ingredients.
Taste and adjust the seasoning, adding more salt or lime juice if needed.
Refrigerate the Tomatillo Salsa for at least 30 minutes to allow the flavors to meld.
Serve the salsa as a dip with tortilla chips, as a topping for tacos, grilled meats, or any dish that could use a zesty and tangy kick.

Enjoy the fresh and tangy flavor of Tomatillo Salsa, a versatile and delicious condiment in Mexican cuisine!

Salads:

Grilled Chicken and Avocado Salad

Ingredients:

For the Grilled Chicken:

- 2 boneless, skinless chicken breasts
- 2 tablespoons olive oil
- 1 teaspoon ground cumin
- 1 teaspoon paprika
- Salt and black pepper, to taste

For the Salad:

- 6 cups mixed salad greens (lettuce, spinach, arugula, etc.)
- 1 cup cherry tomatoes, halved
- 1 cucumber, sliced
- 1 red bell pepper, sliced
- 1/2 red onion, thinly sliced
- 2 avocados, sliced

For the Dressing:

- 1/4 cup olive oil
- 2 tablespoons balsamic vinegar
- 1 teaspoon Dijon mustard
- 1 clove garlic, minced
- Salt and black pepper, to taste

Instructions:

Preheat the grill or grill pan to medium-high heat.
In a bowl, mix olive oil, ground cumin, paprika, salt, and black pepper. Coat the chicken breasts with the spice mixture.

Grill the chicken breasts for about 6-8 minutes per side, or until they are fully cooked and have nice grill marks. Cooking time may vary depending on the thickness of the chicken breasts.

Remove the chicken from the grill and let it rest for a few minutes before slicing it into strips.

In a large salad bowl, combine mixed salad greens, cherry tomatoes, cucumber, red bell pepper, red onion, and sliced avocados.

In a small bowl, whisk together olive oil, balsamic vinegar, Dijon mustard, minced garlic, salt, and black pepper to create the dressing.

Pour the dressing over the salad and toss gently to coat the ingredients.

Arrange the grilled chicken strips on top of the salad.

Serve the Grilled Chicken and Avocado Salad immediately, and enjoy a flavorful and healthy meal.

This salad is not only delicious but also provides a good balance of protein, healthy fats, and fresh vegetables. Customize it with your favorite salad ingredients and enjoy a satisfying and nutritious dish!

Nopales (Cactus) Salad

Ingredients:

- 2 nopales (cactus pads)
- 1 tablespoon olive oil
- 1 clove garlic, minced
- Salt and black pepper, to taste
- 1 cup cherry tomatoes, halved
- 1/2 red onion, thinly sliced
- 1 jalapeño, seeded and finely chopped
- 1/4 cup fresh cilantro, chopped
- Juice of 1 lime
- 1 tablespoon extra-virgin olive oil
- Queso fresco or feta cheese, crumbled (optional, for garnish)

Instructions:

Using a sharp knife, carefully remove the thorns and edges from the nopales. Rinse them under cold water.

In a pot of boiling water, blanch the nopales for about 5 minutes. Drain and rinse under cold water to stop the cooking process.

In a skillet, heat olive oil over medium heat. Add minced garlic and sauté for about 1 minute until fragrant.

Add the blanched nopales to the skillet, season with salt and black pepper, and sauté for another 5-7 minutes, or until they are tender. Allow them to cool.

Slice the cooked nopales into strips.

In a large bowl, combine the sliced nopales, cherry tomatoes, red onion, jalapeño, and chopped cilantro.

In a small bowl, whisk together lime juice and extra-virgin olive oil to create the dressing.

Pour the dressing over the salad and toss gently to coat.

Optional: Garnish the Nopales Salad with crumbled queso fresco or feta cheese. Refrigerate the salad for at least 30 minutes before serving to allow the flavors to meld.

Serve this Nopales Salad as a refreshing and unique side dish, or as a topping for tacos or grilled meats. Enjoy the bright and zesty flavors of this cactus salad!

Black Bean and Corn Salad

Ingredients:

- 1 can (15 ounces) black beans, drained and rinsed
- 1 cup corn kernels (fresh, frozen, or canned)
- 1 red bell pepper, diced
- 1/2 red onion, finely chopped
- 1 cup cherry tomatoes, halved
- 1/4 cup fresh cilantro, chopped
- Juice of 2 limes
- 3 tablespoons extra-virgin olive oil
- 1 teaspoon ground cumin
- 1 teaspoon chili powder
- Salt and black pepper, to taste
- Avocado slices (optional, for garnish)

Instructions:

In a large bowl, combine black beans, corn kernels, diced red bell pepper, chopped red onion, cherry tomatoes, and chopped cilantro.
In a small bowl, whisk together lime juice, extra-virgin olive oil, ground cumin, chili powder, salt, and black pepper to create the dressing.
Pour the dressing over the salad ingredients.
Toss the salad gently until all the ingredients are well coated with the dressing.
Adjust the seasoning to taste, adding more salt or lime juice if needed.
Cover the bowl and refrigerate the Black Bean and Corn Salad for at least 30 minutes to allow the flavors to meld.
Optional: Garnish with avocado slices just before serving.

Serve this Black Bean and Corn Salad as a refreshing and nutritious side dish, or enjoy it as a light and flavorful lunch. It's perfect for picnics, barbecues, or any occasion where you want a vibrant and tasty dish!

Roasted Poblano Potato Salad

Ingredients:

- 2 pounds potatoes (red or Yukon gold), scrubbed and cut into bite-sized pieces
- 2 poblano peppers
- 1/2 cup mayonnaise
- 1/4 cup sour cream
- 2 tablespoons fresh lime juice
- 1 clove garlic, minced
- 1/4 cup fresh cilantro, chopped
- Salt and black pepper, to taste
- 1/2 cup red onion, finely chopped
- 1/2 cup celery, finely chopped (optional for added crunch)
- 1/2 cup corn kernels (fresh, frozen, or canned)
- 1/2 cup cotija cheese, crumbled (optional, for garnish)
- Additional cilantro for garnish

Instructions:

Preheat the broiler in your oven.
Place poblano peppers on a baking sheet and broil, turning occasionally, until the skin is blistered and charred. This usually takes about 5-7 minutes.
Remove the poblano peppers from the oven and place them in a bowl. Cover the bowl with plastic wrap and let them steam for about 10 minutes. This makes it easier to peel the skin.
After steaming, peel the skin off the poblano peppers, remove the seeds, and chop them into small pieces.
In a large pot, boil the potato pieces until they are fork-tender. Drain and let them cool slightly.
In a large mixing bowl, whisk together mayonnaise, sour cream, lime juice, minced garlic, chopped cilantro, salt, and black pepper.
Add the chopped poblano peppers, red onion, celery (if using), and corn to the bowl. Mix well.
Add the cooked and slightly cooled potatoes to the bowl. Gently toss until the potatoes are evenly coated with the dressing.
Refrigerate the Roasted Poblano Potato Salad for at least 1-2 hours before serving to allow the flavors to meld.

Just before serving, garnish with crumbled cotija cheese and additional cilantro.

Enjoy this Roasted Poblano Potato Salad as a flavorful and slightly spicy side dish for your summer gatherings or barbecues!

Jicama and Mango Slaw

Ingredients:

- 1 medium-sized jicama, peeled and julienned
- 1 ripe mango, peeled, pitted, and julienned
- 1 red bell pepper, thinly sliced
- 1/2 red onion, thinly sliced
- 1/4 cup fresh cilantro, chopped
- Juice of 2 limes
- 2 tablespoons honey or maple syrup
- 2 tablespoons olive oil
- Salt and black pepper, to taste
- Chili powder or Tajín (optional, for a hint of spice)

Instructions:

In a large bowl, combine jicama, mango, red bell pepper, red onion, and chopped cilantro.

In a small bowl, whisk together lime juice, honey or maple syrup, olive oil, salt, and black pepper to create the dressing.

Pour the dressing over the jicama and mango mixture.

Toss the slaw gently until all the ingredients are well coated with the dressing.

Optional: Sprinkle chili powder or Tajín over the slaw for a hint of spice.

Refrigerate the Jicama and Mango Slaw for at least 30 minutes before serving to allow the flavors to meld.

Serve the slaw as a refreshing side dish, topping for tacos, or a light and healthy snack.

This Jicama and Mango Slaw is perfect for warm weather, providing a burst of flavors and textures. Enjoy the crispness of jicama and the sweetness of mango in every bite!

Appetizers and Snacks:

Tres Leches Cake

Ingredients:

For the Cake:

- 1 cup all-purpose flour
- 1 1/2 teaspoons baking powder
- 1/4 teaspoon salt
- 4 large eggs, separated
- 1 cup granulated sugar
- 1/3 cup whole milk
- 1 teaspoon vanilla extract

For the Three Milks Mixture:

- 1 can (14 ounces) sweetened condensed milk
- 1 can (12 ounces) evaporated milk
- 1 cup whole milk

For the Whipped Cream Topping:

- 1 cup heavy cream
- 2 tablespoons powdered sugar
- 1 teaspoon vanilla extract

Instructions:

Preheat your oven to 350°F (175°C). Grease and flour a 9x13-inch baking pan.
In a medium bowl, whisk together the flour, baking powder, and salt.
In a separate large bowl, beat the egg yolks with sugar until light and fluffy. Add the milk and vanilla extract, and mix well.
Gradually add the dry ingredients to the egg yolk mixture, stirring until just combined.
In a clean, dry bowl, beat the egg whites until stiff peaks form.

Gently fold the beaten egg whites into the batter until well combined.

Pour the batter into the prepared baking pan and smooth the top.

Bake in the preheated oven for 25-30 minutes or until a toothpick inserted into the center comes out clean.

While the cake is baking, prepare the three milks mixture. In a bowl, whisk together the sweetened condensed milk, evaporated milk, and whole milk.

Once the cake is out of the oven, let it cool for about 10 minutes. Use a fork or skewer to poke holes all over the cake.

Pour the three milks mixture evenly over the warm cake, allowing it to absorb the liquid.

Let the cake cool to room temperature, then refrigerate for at least 2 hours or overnight to allow the flavors to meld.

Before serving, make the whipped cream topping. In a chilled bowl, beat the heavy cream until soft peaks form. Add powdered sugar and vanilla extract, and continue to beat until stiff peaks form.

Spread the whipped cream over the chilled cake.

Optional: Garnish with a sprinkle of cinnamon or fresh fruit before serving.

Slice and serve this delicious Tres Leches Cake cold. It's a rich and indulgent dessert that's sure to be a hit!

Sopapillas with Honey

Ingredients:

- 2 cups all-purpose flour
- 1 teaspoon baking powder
- 1/2 teaspoon salt
- 2 tablespoons sugar
- 2 tablespoons vegetable oil
- 3/4 cup warm water
- Vegetable oil for frying
- Honey for drizzling

Instructions:

In a large mixing bowl, whisk together the flour, baking powder, salt, and sugar.
Add the vegetable oil to the dry ingredients and mix well.
Gradually add the warm water to the mixture, stirring continuously until a soft dough forms.
Knead the dough on a floured surface until it becomes smooth. Cover the dough with a damp cloth and let it rest for about 15-20 minutes.
Heat vegetable oil in a deep fryer or a large, deep pan to 375°F (190°C).
Roll out the dough on a floured surface to about 1/8 inch thickness.
Cut the dough into squares or triangles. You can use a knife or a pizza cutter for this.
Carefully place a few pieces of the dough into the hot oil, frying until they puff up and turn golden brown. This usually takes about 1-2 minutes per side.
Use a slotted spoon to remove the sopapillas from the oil and place them on paper towels to absorb any excess oil.
Drizzle honey over the warm sopapillas while they are still fresh from the fryer.
Repeat the process until all the sopapillas are fried and coated in honey.
Serve the sopapillas warm and enjoy!

Sopapillas are best served fresh and warm. The crispy, fried dough paired with the sweetness of honey makes for a delicious treat. You can also sprinkle them with cinnamon sugar for an extra layer of flavor.

Mexican Chocolate Brownies

Ingredients:

- 1 cup (2 sticks) unsalted butter
- 1 cup granulated sugar
- 1 cup brown sugar, packed
- 4 large eggs
- 1 teaspoon vanilla extract
- 1 cup all-purpose flour
- 1/2 cup cocoa powder
- 1/2 teaspoon ground cinnamon
- 1/4 teaspoon cayenne pepper (adjust to taste, for a hint of heat)
- 1/4 teaspoon salt
- 1 cup semisweet or bittersweet chocolate chips
- 1/2 cup chopped nuts (optional)

For Topping (optional):

- Powdered sugar
- Ground cinnamon

Instructions:

Preheat your oven to 350°F (175°C). Grease and flour a 9x13-inch baking pan.
In a medium-sized saucepan, melt the butter over low heat. Remove from heat and let it cool slightly.
In a large mixing bowl, whisk together granulated sugar, brown sugar, eggs, and vanilla extract until well combined.
Gradually add the melted butter to the sugar and egg mixture, stirring continuously.
In a separate bowl, sift together flour, cocoa powder, ground cinnamon, cayenne pepper, and salt.
Gradually add the dry ingredients to the wet ingredients, mixing until just combined.
Fold in the chocolate chips and chopped nuts (if using).
Pour the batter into the prepared baking pan, spreading it evenly.

Bake in the preheated oven for 25-30 minutes or until a toothpick inserted into the center comes out with a few moist crumbs (not wet batter).
Remove from the oven and let the brownies cool in the pan.
Optional: Once cooled, sprinkle the top with powdered sugar and ground cinnamon for a decorative touch.
Cut into squares and enjoy your Mexican Chocolate Brownies!

These brownies have a rich chocolate flavor with a hint of warmth from the cinnamon and cayenne pepper. They are perfect for those who enjoy a combination of sweet and spicy flavors in their desserts.

Prickly Pear Sorbet

Ingredients:

- 4-5 prickly pears
- 1 cup water
- 1 cup granulated sugar
- Juice of 2 limes
- 1-2 tablespoons vodka (optional, to improve texture)
- Mint leaves for garnish (optional)

Instructions:

Prepare the Prickly Pears:
- Wear gloves to handle prickly pears, as they have small thorns.
- Slice off the ends of each prickly pear and make a shallow cut along one side.
- Carefully peel off the skin, revealing the flesh.
- Chop the peeled prickly pears into chunks.

Make Prickly Pear Puree:
- Place the prickly pear chunks in a blender or food processor.
- Blend until you have a smooth puree.
- Strain the puree through a fine mesh sieve to remove the seeds. You should have about 1 cup of prickly pear puree.

Make Simple Syrup:
- In a saucepan, combine water and granulated sugar.
- Heat over medium heat, stirring until the sugar is completely dissolved.
- Allow the simple syrup to cool.

Combine Ingredients:
- In a mixing bowl, combine the prickly pear puree, simple syrup, and lime juice.
- Optionally, add 1-2 tablespoons of vodka to improve the sorbet's texture and prevent it from freezing too hard.

Chill the Mixture:
- Refrigerate the mixture for at least 2-3 hours or until thoroughly chilled.

Freeze in Ice Cream Maker:
- Pour the chilled mixture into an ice cream maker.
- Churn according to the manufacturer's instructions until it reaches a sorbet-like consistency.

Transfer and Freeze:
- Transfer the churned sorbet into a lidded container.
- Freeze for an additional 2-4 hours or until firm.

Serve:
- Scoop the Prickly Pear Sorbet into bowls or cones.
- Garnish with mint leaves if desired.

Enjoy this cooling and vibrant Prickly Pear Sorbet as a delightful dessert on a hot day!

Churro Ice Cream Sandwiches

Ingredients:

For the Churros:

- 1 cup water
- 1/2 cup unsalted butter
- 2 tablespoons granulated sugar
- 1/4 teaspoon salt
- 1 cup all-purpose flour
- 3 large eggs
- Vegetable oil, for frying

For Coating:

- 1/2 cup granulated sugar
- 1 teaspoon ground cinnamon

For Assembly:

- Your favorite ice cream (vanilla, chocolate, or cinnamon-flavored work well)
- Toppings (chocolate sauce, caramel sauce, sprinkles, etc.)

Instructions:

Prepare the Churro Dough:
- In a saucepan, combine water, butter, sugar, and salt. Bring to a boil over medium-high heat.
- Reduce the heat to low and add the flour all at once. Stir vigorously with a wooden spoon until the mixture forms a ball and pulls away from the sides of the pan.
- Remove from heat and let it cool for a couple of minutes.

Add Eggs:
- Add the eggs one at a time, beating well after each addition. The dough should become smooth and glossy.

Heat Oil:

- Heat vegetable oil in a deep fryer or large, deep pan to 375°F (190°C).

Pipe Churros:
- Transfer the churro dough to a piping bag fitted with a star tip.
- Pipe 4-6 inch long churros directly into the hot oil, using scissors or a knife to cut the dough.

Fry Churros:
- Fry the churros until golden brown, turning them as needed to ensure even cooking. This usually takes about 3-4 minutes.

Coat with Cinnamon-Sugar:
- In a shallow dish, mix together granulated sugar and ground cinnamon.
- While the churros are still warm, roll them in the cinnamon-sugar mixture until well coated.

Let Churros Cool:
- Allow the coated churros to cool slightly.

Assemble Ice Cream Sandwiches:
- Once the churros are cool enough to handle but still warm, slice them in half horizontally.
- Place a scoop of your favorite ice cream between two churro halves.

Add Toppings:
- Optionally, roll the edges of the ice cream sandwiches in additional toppings like sprinkles or chopped nuts.

Serve Immediately:
- Serve the Churro Ice Cream Sandwiches immediately, and enjoy the crispy, cinnamon-sugar exterior paired with the creamy ice cream!

These Churro Ice Cream Sandwiches are a delightful treat for any occasion, combining the classic flavors of churros and ice cream into one delicious dessert.

Anise Seed Bizcochitos

Ingredients:

- 1 cup (2 sticks) unsalted butter, softened
- 1 cup granulated sugar
- 2 large eggs
- 1 teaspoon anise extract
- 3 cups all-purpose flour
- 2 teaspoons baking powder
- 1/2 teaspoon salt
- 1/4 cup brandy or whiskey
- 1 teaspoon ground cinnamon (for coating)
- 1/4 cup granulated sugar (for coating)

Instructions:

Preheat the Oven:
- Preheat your oven to 350°F (175°C). Line baking sheets with parchment paper.

Cream Butter and Sugar:
- In a large bowl, cream together the softened butter and granulated sugar until light and fluffy.

Add Eggs and Anise Extract:
- Beat in the eggs, one at a time, until well incorporated. Add the anise extract and mix until combined.

Combine Dry Ingredients:
- In a separate bowl, whisk together the flour, baking powder, and salt.

Mix Dough:
- Gradually add the dry ingredients to the butter mixture, mixing until the dough comes together.

Add Brandy:
- Pour in the brandy or whiskey and mix until the dough is smooth.

Roll and Cut:
- On a floured surface, roll out the dough to about 1/4 inch thickness. Use cookie cutters to cut out shapes.

Prepare Cinnamon-Sugar Coating:
- In a small bowl, mix together the ground cinnamon and granulated sugar.

Coat Cookies:

- Lightly coat each cookie with the cinnamon-sugar mixture.

Bake:
- Place the coated cookies on the prepared baking sheets and bake in the preheated oven for 10-12 minutes or until the edges are lightly golden.

Cool:
- Allow the bizcochitos to cool on the baking sheets for a few minutes before transferring them to a wire rack to cool completely.

Serve and Enjoy:
- Once cooled, serve these Anise Seed Bizcochitos with your favorite hot beverage or share them during festive occasions.

The combination of anise and cinnamon gives these cookies a unique and delightful flavor. Enjoy these Anise Seed Bizcochitos as a special treat with friends and family!

Flan with Caramel Sauce

Ingredients:

For the Caramel Sauce:

- 1 cup granulated sugar
- 1/4 cup water

For the Flan:

- 4 large eggs
- 1 can (14 ounces) sweetened condensed milk
- 1 can (12 ounces) evaporated milk
- 1 tablespoon vanilla extract

Instructions:

1. Preheat the Oven:

- Preheat your oven to 350°F (175°C).

2. Make the Caramel Sauce:

- In a saucepan, combine granulated sugar and water over medium heat.
- Stir until the sugar dissolves, then let it simmer without stirring.
- Swirl the pan occasionally to ensure even caramelization.
- Cook until the syrup turns a deep amber color. Be cautious not to burn it.
- Once the desired color is reached, immediately pour the caramel into the bottom of a baking dish or individual ramekins, swirling to coat the bottom evenly.

3. Prepare the Flan Mixture:

- In a bowl, whisk together eggs, sweetened condensed milk, evaporated milk, and vanilla extract until well combined.

4. Strain the Mixture:

- Strain the flan mixture through a fine-mesh sieve to ensure a smooth texture.

5. Pour into the Baking Dish:

- Pour the strained flan mixture over the caramel layer in the baking dish or ramekins.

6. Create a Water Bath:

- Place the baking dish or ramekins in a larger baking pan. Fill the larger pan with hot water until it reaches halfway up the sides of the smaller dish or ramekins. This creates a water bath for baking the flan.

7. Bake:

- Bake in the preheated oven for approximately 50-60 minutes or until the flan is set around the edges but slightly jiggly in the center.

8. Cool and Refrigerate:

- Allow the flan to cool to room temperature in the water bath.
- Once cooled, cover and refrigerate for at least 4 hours or overnight to set.

9. Serve:

- To serve, run a knife around the edges of the flan to loosen it.
- Invert the flan onto a serving plate, allowing the caramel to drizzle over the top.

Enjoy this delicious and velvety Flan with Caramel Sauce as a delightful ending to your meals!